In John Kropf's first collection of poetry, the images may come from the Midwest, but the sentiments are universal. An adult remembering boyhood realizes that we never know when it will be the last time we play in the yard. "Hometown" assures us that memories never fade: they are "right where I left them." Even what we discard carries its weight: in "The End of History," trash becomes our "discarded histories." In subsequent sections of the book, the images go farther afield. "Lost City" shows us the point of view of the last inhabitant who leaves, "turning that city into a tomb," but also that of the first who declares at sunrise that a "hillside would be a city." There is humor here as well: coffee is a dark redeemer from an exotic land, while feet can save your soul. These free verse poems tell of time, memory, boyhood, and the idea that although the past is gone, it is never lost.

—Deborah Fleming, author of *Earthrise*

Whoever you are, in John Kropf's collection, *A Midwestern Heart*, you will find something to identify with or remember. As a former Midwesterner, I recall the long lawns of the Republic I mowed as described in this book, as well as the sense of nearing Winter that summoned me home as a child. But I also, as a city dweller, recall the fantastic poem about entering a Metro station early on a rainy morning, as well as the humorous poem about dry cleaning that compares it to Sisyphus' punishment, "repeat for eternity." I believe that anyone who opens this book will find their own touch-points that will vividly bring back a moment of time, a bit of personal history. And it's all written with a practiced hand that captures the Midwest beautifully, accurately, and with as much as heart as the poet could give.

—Donald Illich, author of *Chance Bodies*

## Other Books by John Kropf

*Color Capital of the World: Growing Up with the Legacy of a Crayon Company* (Series on Ohio History and Culture) (University of Akron Press, 2022).

*Unknown Sands: Journeys Around the World's Most Isolated Country* (Dusty Spark Publishing, 2006).

## Bottom Dog Press

Huron, Ohio

# A Midwestern Heart

## John Kropf

Harmony Series

Copyright © 2024
John Kropf and Bottom Dog Press
All rights reserved.
This book, or parts thereof, may not be reproduced in any form without permission from the publisher; exceptions are made for brief excerpts used in published reviews.

ISBN: 978-1-947504-44-8
Bottom Dog Press, Inc.
PO Box 425, Huron, OH 44839
Lsmithdog@aol.com
http://smithdocs.net

Credits:
General Editor: Larry Smith
Cover & Layout Design, Editing: Susanna Sharp-Schwacke
Editorial Assistance, Copy Editing: Dona McCormack
Cover Image: Rob Evans, *Marietta Train II*,
digital painting, ©1994
Title Page Graphics: Molly Stewart

## Contents

### I. Childhood

| | |
|---|---|
| Back Yard | 9 |
| A Boy's Lost Instructions | 10 |
| The Last Day of Childhood | 12 |
| Working with the Elements | 14 |
| Cloudy Days | 15 |
| Hometown | 16 |
| Summer 1969 | 17 |
| TV Test Pattern | 19 |
| Wild Town | 20 |

### II. Seasons

| | |
|---|---|
| The Hill of Perception | 23 |
| Change of Seasons | 24 |
| A Midwestern Boy Mows the Fields of the Republic | 25 |
| Winter Side of Fall | 26 |
| Ghosts of Early December | 27 |
| Fair Weather Friend | 28 |

### III. Work

| | |
|---|---|
| Vienna Metro Station, December 9, 6:38 am | 31 |
| The End of History | 32 |
| Five Tales of Dry Cleaning | 33 |
| Pinstripe Uprising | 35 |
| Investing Wisely | 36 |
| Escape to Return | 37 |
| On Farragut Square | 38 |
| *Your Call is Very Important to Us* | 39 |

### IV. Stories

| | |
|---|---|
| An Elegy to the American Crayon Company | 43 |
| Lost City | 44 |
| Coffee, Your History | 45 |
| Abandoned Memory | 46 |
| Moral Footing | 47 |

| | |
|---|---:|
| OPPOSITE DAY | 48 |
| MEDITATIONS AT MCDONALDS | 49 |
| SELLING YOUR LIFE | 50 |

## V. Travel

| | |
|---|---:|
| BEAUTY SUBSTITUTIONS | 53 |
| CONTINENTAL DRIFT | 54 |
| EVERYWHERE YOU ARE AND MORE | 55 |
| SECOND STORY MYSTERY | 56 |
| WHAT LIES AHEAD | 57 |
| SHADOWS OF THE ROAD | 58 |
| WESTERLY COURSE | 59 |

## VI. Time

| | |
|---|---:|
| TAKE *THAT*, TIME | 63 |
| TIME NOT REMEMBERED | 64 |
| THREE WORLDS OF MEMORY | 65 |
| TIME VALUE | 67 |
| FUTURE MADMAN | 68 |
| KNOW TIME LIKE THE PRESENT | 69 |
| HUMAN AUTUMN: A CENTO | 70 |

## VII. Penny Arcade

| | |
|---|---:|
| DESOLATION HAIKU | 73 |
| PLASTIC GROCERY BAG | 74 |
| IRONY OF LOYALTY | 75 |
| SPECTATOR OF INVERSE PROPORTIONS | 76 |
| NOT MYSELF | 77 |
| OUT OF ORDER | 78 |
| TWO CAT POEM | 79 |
| SCENES FROM A STORMY NIGHT | 80 |
| APPROACHING A SHORT POEM | 81 |
| MADHOUSE: A CENTO | 82 |
| MATCHMAKING CHALLENGE | 83 |
| DIGITAL HAIKU | 84 |

| | |
|---|---:|
| ABOUT THE AUTHOR | 85 |

# I. Childhood

# Back Yard

Everyone should have a back yard
at least once in life.
You can dig to China,
play badminton,
tend to your hydrangeas,
pitch a tent,
and camp out with your best friend.
In summer, you can sunbathe with a cool drink,
and if you wait long enough,
watch stars and galaxies reveal themselves.
In fall, you can rake leaves
and send them back into the sky
with fire
And if you ever dig all the way to China
you could end up in someone's back yard.

# A Boy's Lost Instructions

*There was a final time when you said,*
*"I'm going out to play," but never realized it was final...*

1. Parachute Man

My grandfather floated above the earth
in the wicker basket of an Army balloon
to watch the Kaiser's army in World War I,
but then fell to earth in a parachute.
Fifty years later
he stood in our back yard
and taught me how to make a parachute man
with a handkerchief, string and a lead sinker.
You folded the handkerchief in squares
and tossed your parachute man into the air.

Nowadays most men don't carry handkerchiefs.

2. Talking to Kites

My father showed me how to send messages
up to kites in the March skies of northern Ohio.
He used old memo pads with his company logo
and we'd write notes,
"How are things up there?" then
tear and tape the sheets around the kite string.
He'd give it a slide up the line
and off it would go, spinning around till the message was
delivered.

Today's stunt kite flyer would not sit still long enough
to send a message.

3. Burning Buildings

In the fall
we would burn piles of leaves.
My father would clean old boxes from the garage
and use his pocketknife to cut out doors, windows,
and a hole for a cardboard tube chimney.
He set the box on top of the burning leaves
'till the flames flickered inside the windows
and smoke billowed from the tube,
and watch the box flame into a dark, brittle crust.

4. Backyard Cannon

I can't remember who passed the secret instructions,
but it was known among boys my age and time.
Gather four 7UP cans, top and bottom,
connect to a long stick,
load with a tennis ball,
fuel with lighter fluid,
and with the right technique,
fire tennis balls into the air and over your house.
Today the neighbors would call the cops
and put you on a list.

## The Last Day of Childhood

Our Friends would marvel
at two rope swings hung from the rafters,
one thousand feet of newsprint slung on a spool,
the bucket on the floor held sticks of crayons

Supplies to build great structures of the world:
Legos, Tinkertoys, and Lincoln Logs
carried by caravans of Tonka Trucks.

Superior to the Bodleian Library:
picture books on geography, WWII, treasures of the art world,
American history and Charles Addams cartoons.
Archives of Donald Duck, Batman and Archie comics
    —selected by my sister,
    —bought by my mother,
    —read my me,
    —and hauled away by my father.

Off in the forbidden realms:
my grandfather's workbench
and its cast iron vice
clenched and healed
dolls, bikes and chairs.

In the opposing corner
whiteness and humming
of an ever industrious
washer and dryer
gurgling and rumbling.
In dark rivers below
lies the crocodile of a sump pump.

Tucked in a recess
like a scarab beetle,
a dusty old bowling trophy.
A royal chamber
enshrines artifacts as sacred
as treasures from Tutankhamun's tomb.
And now as distant as the buried bones of a lost caravan.

When we left the house,
my father inscribed our story
in his own hieroglyphics
on the center basement beam,
abandoned to later civilizations.

*This house was built in 1961, by Tom Krammer for Walter and Mary Kropf, daughter Ann (born 1959) and son, John (born September 1961.) It was also home to various and sundry dogs and cats, guinea pigs, mice, turtles and a parrot named Hoffman.*

## Working with the Elements

Night and awake in bed,
I hear voices outside,
voices of 14-year-olds,
voices that belonged to me 30 years ago.

The time when you have never felt
so carefree, so cool, so immortal,
everything in life before you,
and you barely recognize this.

The 14-year-olds fill their senses
with deep hues of the northern latitudes,
and the energy and ozone of the big lake.

I can't go outside and join them.
It's not my time,
but hearing voices and waves
is the nearest thing to time travel.

I see myself at a bonfire on the beach,
maybe flirting with a girl
under the same constellations,
absorbing the same light and water.

My daughter is out there
in the darkness,
the old elements firmly embedded in her.

## Cloudy Days

Because we cannot talk anymore,
I send you a cloud,
and in conversation
you send one back.
Our talk could be anything
from sleek stratus in the morning
to a flotilla of billowing cumulus
in the afternoon

My favorites are Saturdays.
If the sky is blue
I send high-flying streaks of cirrus
and you answer at sunset
with impeccable timing
in red-orange nimbus
backlit in gold.

I'm always watching the sky.

# Hometown

No one is left in my hometown.
My people are gone.

But my memories are there
right where I left them,
wandering streets, schools, and fields.

I could revive the spirit of the place,
but what would that matter now?

My route is now reversed,
what was once a destination
became the hometown,
and now the old hometown
is just another destination.

I still drive the Ohio Turnpike,
and near Exit Seven I sense
an urge of memories
tugging from across dark fields
to the north.

# Summer 1969

June

In broad daylight
I crashed my Matchbox Ferraris
on homemade gravel roads.
Saturday nights,
the thunder of stock car engines
traveled miles across cornfields,
the blacktop oval and Doppler
making their revolutions rise and fall
like the din of a faraway battle.
The thunder lasted a thousand summers,
or maybe just five or six.

July

My parents' guests laughed and drank
on the patio under the shadows
of an 80-year-old oak tree spared by the contractor,
leaving it encircled
like a Druid meeting place.
When humans cast their shadows
on the moon for the first time,
I ran from our black and white TV
to the patio with urgent dispatches:
"The Eagle has landed."
"Stepping off the LEM now…"
Not one Christopher Columbus among the guests
came to the TV with me.

August

An hour ago
it was the afternoon hum of a lawn mower
marching up and down the yard
spinning silver steel against green grass,
but now I sprawl out on the lawn
listening to the transient drone
of an unseen plane
following a carefree flight plan
threshing its blade through the hot blue sky
and gone.

# TV Test Pattern

It was the end,
back when TV stations
shut off and went to bed
like the rest of the civilized world.

I would watch until
the last of the late, late movies ended.
Some showed the star-spangled banner,
others the pilot having touched the hand of God.

I looked on helpless
until my last companion turned away,
posting a sign on the door,
a test pattern of lines and numbers
commanded by a determined Indian in a headdress.

I knew it was the end,
because after one last desperate
twist of the channel dial,
there was desolation,
and off I went to dream
under a blanket of static white.

## Wild Town

I ran wild
then ran away
from a northern Ohio town,
but I took the town
and my wild ways with me.

## II. Seasons

## The Hill of Perception

There's a hill in northern Michigan
where summer twilight lasts so long
that day forgets to leave until
well after night's arrival.

Shadows depart for the western horizon,
blue waters bleed into purple shore,
and sky melts into earth.

Boundaries are blurred,
waking-dozing border crossings
between reality and dreams.

## Change of Seasons

In the bungalows of happiness,
householders put up their
canned goods of well-wishes.

Out back, in derelict steel drums,
the kids stoke
bonfires of resentment.

At the end of the street,
darkness and winter
are waiting.

## A Midwestern Boy Mows the Fields of the Republic

I mow my lawn
in shrinking concentric squares,
like a disappearing island.
But no lawn is an island.
Why not push past my boundaries
to the neighbor's yard?

I'll need time off from work
as I race up and down
suburban streets
connecting rivers of lawn
with the Capital lawn.
New England town greens
and Kentucky bluegrass,
each require a stately pace
to please pampered thoroughbreds.

Midwest 100-yard coliseums
require a precision coif,
no dreams in artificial turf.
Is it any wonder why it was abandoned
and returned to earth?

My vast grid extends to summer lawns of memory,
front yards of modest Ohio towns
to the graveyards of my grandparents.
I mow Little League fields in diagonal textures,
the kind you see during the baseball highlights.

I'm left mowing in the dark,
one giant rolling lawn
of the great Republic,
from sea to shining sea.

# Winter Side of Fall

Evening light is best this time of year.
Glow of yellow leaves on trees,
glow of light inside homes,
and glow of the sun's low angle
burn together in a golden hour.
Evening moves on.
Sky orange air
drains into the horizon.
Air, now more cold than cool,
carries the wood-fire smell
known to the most ancient of ancestors,
elements of instinct recognized as a kid
when you look up from down the street,
more night than day,
moved by dying cold-air colors.
Time to find your way home.

## Ghosts of Early December

After the last leaves fall,
hungry ghosts hang
one or two from a tree,
awaiting what the wind brings.

# Fair Weather Friend

*Winter arrives as death,*
*yet when winter departs, does it die?*

That patch of snow,
the last one,
the scab
left over from winter's fight,

arriving at night
as flurries and fanfare,
it disappears in the day,
silently shrunken by the sun.

Once I was against it,
now I'm for it,
because it's the underdog
destined to lose
at the end of the season.

## III. Work

## Vienna Metro Stations, December 9, 6:38AM

Black
at the station,
rain
in a steady stream,
everyone
in layers, hats and hoods.

The platform shows like a congregation
of tenth century monks
in oversized cloaks and cowls,
or battle-weary soldiers laden with gear
waiting to board a landing craft.

Our train arrives,
door chimes,
forming up
under the rain
we board in silence,
delivered to our monasteries and battlefields.

# The End of History

We know
it's trash day eve
when green and blue bins
picket the street
like sentries
posted curbside
to stand watch
through the night
until huge trucks
smash the dawn,
dispatching their commandos
to flip idiot lids,
relieving us
of our discarded histories.

# Five Tales of Dry Cleaning

1. Eastern Mysticism Dry Cleaners

You give,
the cleaner takes.
The cleaner gives,
you take.
Yin and yang,
swirling
in a perfectly-balanced dance
of perpetuity.

2. *Deadliest Catch* Dry Cleaners

You splash your catch
across the Formica slab
like opening trawling nets
hauled from the Bering Sea.
The usual button-downs,
a couple of blue suits,
and a black cocktail dress—
all keepers
to be cleaned and dried,
shrink-wrapped and
displayed on hangers.

3. Greek Tragedy Dry Cleaners

If Sisyphus were alive today,
Zeus would exchange his rock
for dry cleaning.
Drop off the dry cleaning.
Pick up the dry cleaning.
Drop off the dry cleaning.
Pick up the dry cleaning.
...repeat for eternity.

4. Crimes and Misdemeanors Dry Cleaning

You bring in this week's delinquents,
like a bailiff at criminal court.
A dirty and rumpled bunch,
some stained with blood,
some with food,
signs of their crimes
and life on the street.
The cleaner inspects,
counts them off,
and sentence is passed.
On the day of release,
shirts, suits and dresses
stand at attention,
returned and reformed,
ready for polite society.

5. Whimsical Cleaners

Wadded and balled, a disgraceful mess,
six shirts, two suits and your wife's cocktail dress,
counted and inspected for blood and for food,
like clues to a crime that was undoubtedly rude.

They're scooped into sacks and carted away.
You need not worry, you'll see them someday.

On your return, round and round the carousel goes,
and where it stops will be all your clean clothes.

## Pinstripe Uprising

Stock-straight
pinstripe executives
rise up
on elevators
even straighter
than their suits
or the skyscrapers
lining the avenue
to overlook
the parallels
of the city grid
from on high.

## Investing Wisely

Investors say
my money should have a plan,
work hard for me,
forge a path in the market,
compound, diversify, hedge,
instill confidence
to skipper that 50-foot yacht
under sail toward bright horizons,
steadfast supporter of my dreams.

But my money is lazy.
It slumps down at its desk,
failing to pay attention
like a daydreaming student
at the back of the class.
Late at night
when it thinks I'm not looking,
I can tell that
my money
verges on the irresponsible.
It wants to run away
and join the lottery.

## Escape to Return

I'm that guy
who will plot
a nighttime escape,
dodging the searchlights
to scale the prison wall
for a mad frolic of freedom,
laughing and careening
through city streets.

But I'm also that guy
who will willingly
break back into prison
and slip into my cell
before sunrise.

Years later,
when my sentence is served
and I walk out the prison gates,
I'll secretly savor the wild time
even more.

## On Farragut Square

As daylight turns to darkness,
manmade lights turn on
along the avenue.
There stands Admiral Farragut,
a statue silhouetted high on his plinth
because he sent his fleet forward,
damning the torpedoes.

It's about this time that
fleets of FedEx and UPS trucks arrive
around his square, damning the traffic
to double-park, load their cargoes,
and sail into the sea of highways
on an evening breeze.

## Your Call is Very Important to Us

I know they think
of little else but
my call,

so important that
it can't be trusted
to unreliable humans.

Computer generated,
almost-human
transmissions of delivered
sincerity.

That's the sound of
automated caring.

# IV. Stories

## An Elegy to the American Crayon Company

Crumbling black brick
with white lettering,
index-finger smokestack,
dismantled machines,
lost workers—all
instruments of color creation.
Kindergarten perceptions
of broccoli-stalk trees and beaming suns.
An artist's rendering of gauzy scenes
of a Bordeaux countryside.
Cylinders of orange, mauve and maroon
poured, molded, dried
cut, packaged, and shipped.
Opened in rooms of A, B, C, 1, 2, 3,
and abandoned on a June afternoon.
A worn palette of nubs
rolling around
in a busted box.

# Lost City

To the untrained eye
it was nothing.
But when I heard they found the lost city
covered in the sands of the high desert,
I thought of the last inhabitant
on his last night ,
warmed by dark star embers
inside the city walls,
and how at sunrise
he walked out of the dusty ruins
into the morning sun,
turning the city into a tomb.

But then I have to think
of the first person
on his first night,
who camped above the riverbank
on a fertile hillside,
tracing the white stars
into constellations,
and declared at sunrise that
this hillside would be a city.

## Coffee, Your History

Dark redeemer,
carrying legends of Sumatra, Arabia, Columbia.

Creator of cultures,
fuel for a Sufi's whirling dance,
drink of protests by patriots
in the days of revolution,
drunk in heroic proportions
by Balzac and Beats
made mad by your power.

Drunk black
by my father
on the troop ship,
far side of the Pacific,
World War II,
because green skin of slime congealed
on tins of curdled cream.

The history
of why I drink you as I do.

## Abandoned Memory

Feet crunch on glass
in an abandoned house.
In a ray of light
something still glitters,
beautiful upon the floor.

## Moral Footing

Tenderfoots haven't walked
enough to know.
Feet stomp grapes under the Tuscan sun.
Step across the threshold.
Kick victory through the uprights.
Take premiere position during *Swan Lake*.
Walk hot coals to prove
the mind can take it.
Surfers hang ten
in blue Hawaii.
Robinson Crusoe finds hope
in Friday's footprint.
History holds feet accountable:
don't tread on me,
goose step down the Champs-Élysées,
march across a bridge in Selma.
Feet can save your souls.

# Opposite Day

On Opposite Day,
lawyers do their best to forgive their adversaries
and let bygones be bygones.

Engineers let the metaphors and alliterations flow
from their mechanical pencils.

Poets strictly obey the rules of grammar and syntax,
limiting their words to factual narratives of a mathematical
        nature.

Casino bosses allow the blackjack players
to have a do-over if they like.

Auditors do a few back-of-the-envelope estimates and figure
that's good enough for Corporate's fiscal year.

Auto mechanics forgo replacing the disc brakes on that
Econoline Van and cry
over how to save its soul in the afterlife.

Preachers preach their hunches on five-card stud
and draw for an inside straight.

Clowns keep one to a car and maintain a safe distance.
giving each other plenty of time to exit with dignity.

Talk show hosts invite philosophers on
to have that long metaphysical discourse.

Comedians decide irony has no place on stage
with their monologues of tragedy.

Everyone needs an opposite day once in a while.

# Meditations at McDonalds

At McDonalds
everyone is warned:
*The coffee is hot.*
It's no different
at my neighborhood McDonalds,
except you don't have to worry.
Friends reserve a table,
like the gray hairs in navy windbreakers
from the Korean War
who come to talk
next to the Latina mothers
and their toddlers' Happy Meals,
and an Asian woman
bundled against the cold and old age
holding her cane like a scepter
while collecting greetings
from the sanitation crew
trimmed in their vestments
of neon yellow.
The red Coke dispenser
froths away behind
two men alternating
between Arabic and English
sitting on avocado and purple upholstered seats,
as if the place needed to be brightened up.

## Selling Your Life

If you had to sell your life story as a best-selling book,
could you write your history through
    —the places you called home,
    —the schools that educated you,
    —the cars you owned,
    —every girl you ever kissed,
    —every job you ever worked,
    —and any good deed you did?

But if you did, who would want to read about you?
Instead, could you write about
    —the landlords that had you evicted,
    —the schools that expelled you,
    —the cars you crashed,
    —every girl who ever dumped you,
    —the bosses who fired you,
    —and your time in prison?

Good guys and success.
Bad guys and failure.
More people read the *Inferno* than *Paradiso*
and look at Goofus before Gallant.
I always read villains first.

# V. Travel

## Beauty Substitutions

On a slate-gray February evening
when you can't find beauty
from the Amtrak window
in the black eyes of derelict buildings,
can you make beauty substitutions?

The rusting steel bones of
a northern New Jersey salvage yard
by twilight
never looked better.

# Continental Drift

Australia is a country,
is an island,
is a continent,
like a whole whale fish
swimming toward
shapely South America,
who looks east
at her heavy-set sister Africa,
indifferent to the chubby bouncing Buddha
Asia swinging its Kamchatka tassel,
balanced on a slender high-heeled Malaysian peninsula
while kicking up an ungainly
Arabian Dutch clog
and shaking his Himalayan girth
in a wild waltz
with the baroque lady of Europe.
Rough and ready North America
eyes the mismatched couple,
cracking the whip of his Aleutian braid
and coiling the overgrown prehensile tail
of Mexico in the warm waters below,
leaving Antarctica alone
to spin as a top
in its own cold abandon.

## Everywhere You Are and More

A short bus ride away
from world's end
and around the block
from the empty quarter
lies the last strip mall,
complete with nail salon,
mattress store, and dry cleaner.

# Second Story Mystery

All I remember
is living on the second floor,
the one you look at from a passing car
on an urban highway
and wonder who lives up there
with the light on
so late at night.
Well, it's me
watching the cars go by,
until one night
driving home from my shift
at the liquor store,
I run out of gas
on some other urban highway,
and there it is
above the rusting guardrail,
a light from a second story window
and me
wondering
who is up there
so late at night
with the light on.

## What Lies Ahead

*Inspired by Loren Eiseley's "All the Strange Hours"*

A harsh wind cuts through the doorway,
the train picking up speed
for the storm-filled country ahead.
Fields and bridges flash by.
The train whistle wails
over the desolate countryside.

Two of us in the boxcar,
alternatively inhabiting the mind
of the other,
thinking about what towns lie ahead.

## Shadows of the Road

Longleaf pines conspire
to strike the road
with slatted shadows,
an off-kilter picket fence
pointing to the setting sun.

# Westerly Course

Driving west
into an unknown country
is a deliberate mystery.
You don't know
what you'll need
or what you'll find on the radio.
The land pushes up green waves
and sand hills
where birds hide
during the day
and you hear them
at night.
At the end
is the ocean
where the sun says,
"Enough—time to
sit still on the shore
and let the waves do the talking."

# VI. Time

## Take *That*, Time

Time won't come out to play.
It won't bargain
for a return trip
or make an exchange of
…a year, a week, a day
for any reason,
no matter how devout.

Wrongly condemned prisoners,
released after decades,
must hate time
for not opening up
and giving back
what everyone agrees
should not have been taken.

Or a persistent old scientist rediscovers
a forgotten element
he once encountered as a young lab assistant,
the one that could have made all the difference to his life
        experiment.

Killjoy time
has firm rules against a do-over.
And I suppose it likes having sayings written about itself…
"If I knew now what I knew then…"
"Making up for lost time…"

Since time won't play along,
I compensate in the present,
willing as much experience
as the moments will allow.

## Time Not Remembered

Down a nameless street
in a forgotten part of town,
behind gray granite walls
and a padlocked gate,
lies a dusty courtyard
in pale light,
with brittle brown leaves
swept into a corner
long ago
by the last gust of wind
from an abandoned age.

# Three Worlds of Memory

Digital:
    Scientists in white lab coats
    engineered a world
    that flawlessly remembers all your inputs,
    your memory outsourced to a secure location
    like what a child thinks heaven is like,
    where you ask God every question you ever wanted.
    Until one day,
    the server crashes
    or power is lost,
    and the screen goes dark.

Paper:
    Since the time of the Han
    the sheets have been there,
    reliable, tangible, unfiltered.
    Open to the page
    and the words are the same
    as yesterday,
    the same as today,
    and will be the same tomorrow.
    A dense treatise, today's newspaper, a 3x5 card;
    you carry paper memory like a security blanket.
    until one day
    you misplace it
    and it gathers dust on a shelf.

Biological:
    You and your synapses are
    the ever-present device.
    You could be naked on a desert island
    and it would be there with you.
    All you need to do
    is exercise its muscles—
    no external source,
    no object to hold,
    nothing to lose,
    till one day
    you forget.

# Time Value

Napoleon said
he could always recover lost space
but never lost time.

Einstein said
you could expand and contract time
like an accordion.

General Hancock ordered the First Minnesota Volunteers
on a suicide charge at Gettysburg—215 casualties of 262 men—
giving him 15 minutes to fill a gap in the Union line.

Vince Lombardi never conceded defeat,
only admitting,
"We ran out of time."

Steven Jobs declared that
the most precious resource
human beings have is time.

This morning,
I hit the snooze button for a handful of minutes
that I'll never remember.

## Future Madman

Your morning visit
with news and coffee,
Past and Present.
Three of you,
here and now,
but always
distractions,
shadows at the door.
It's Future, eternal party crasher,
"Wait, I'll be with you in a second."
"Not a chance," snickers Future,
running down the street
like a Halloween prankster,
laughing like mad.

# Know Time Like the Present

When I call my colleague in Tokyo today
it's tomorrow.
On Saturday
my Sunday *Washington Post* is delivered,
even though it's printed on Thursday.

Twice a year
while you sleep
you can time travel—
spring ahead one hour,
fall back the next.

Tonight,
astronomers can see the light
of the most distant object in the universe
as it appeared 13 billion years ago.
It must be gone by now.

My nine-year-old daughter says,
"Time is made up by people.
What would happen
if we never bothered
to measure it?"

# Human Autumn: A Cento

*All the Strange Hours*, Loren Eiseley

Human autumn
before the snow,
a last attempt to order meaning
before a spring breaks
in the rusted heart
as dreams and memories
fall apart
in irreparable ruin.

Oncoming age
is a vast wild autumn country,
strewn with broken seed pods,
hurrying clouds,
abandoned farm machinery,
and circling crows,
family resemblance
leaping from place to place
across oblivion.

## VII. Penny Arcade Poems

## Desolation Haiku

Balloon in bare tree
black wire hanger in dark closet
frontiers of sadness.

## Plastic Grocery Bag

Is the tumbleweed of the urban landscape,
and sometimes
an undulating jellyfish in a sea of trees.

## Irony of Loyalty

I make my monsters
loyal
while my friends
come and go.

## Spectator of Inverse Proportions

I watched the big game
on the giant screen
with a small mind
and tiny eyes.

## Not Myself

I've been put in this position before,
waking up in the middle of the night
to utter phrases
not my own
(and no one to hear them).

## Out of Order

Old feelings
of young love
came to me
in the first season
as a last resort.

## Two Cat Poem

You lie about
like some corrupt Roman Emperor,
passing judgment
on my every move.

The other of you takes shape as
the household Sphinx,
basking, eyes closed
as I clean out your litter box.

## Scenes from a Stormy Night

The dunce did a dance
with his cup of love.

The fox in the dark
made the house dogs bark.

After the storm,
broken branches
on the black pavement
seem like overgrown tarantulas.

## Approaching a Short Poem

Sit still for me
on the page.
You'll soon be lost
in time.

# **Madhouse: A Cento**

*The Third Coast,* Thomas Dyja

It was a voluntary madhouse,
a museum of expired vices,
a final cry
for ruined lives.

# Matchmaking Challenge

Love tyrant
meets
hermit fanatic.
Oh, what a ride.

## Digital Haiku

Digital morning
Everything needs a password
Everyone forgets.

## About the Author

This is John Kropf's first collection of poetry. He is the author of two previous books, *Color Capital of the World: Growing Up with the Legacy of a Crayon Company*, the story of his family's crayon company in Sandusky, Ohio and winner of Bowling Green State University's 2023 Local History Award, and *Unknown Sands: Travels in the World's Most Isolated Country*. His writing has appeared in *The Washington Post, Baltimore Sun, Middle West Review*, and elsewhere. He is a member of the Society of Midland Authors.

John is a graduate of Denison University with a major in philosophy and earned a law degree and master's degree in public and international affairs from the University of Pittsburgh. He was born and raised in Erie County, Ohio and now works in the Washington, DC, area where he lives with his wife Eileen, and daughter Charlotte.

## Books by Bottom Dog Press

### Harmony Series

*Midwestern Heart: Poems*, John Kropf, 88 pgs., $16
*Tiny Songs: Haiku & Meditations*, by Terry Hermsen, 136 pgs., $16
*Hope as a Construction*, by David Adams, 182 pgs., $18
*Baltic Amber in a Chest: Poems*, by Clarissa Jakobsons, 104 pgs., $16
*Choices: Three Novellas* by Annabel Thomas, 176 pgs., $18
*Pottery Town Blues*, by Karen Kotrba, 128 pgs., $16
*The Pears: Poems*, by Larry Smith, 66 pgs, $15
*Cycling Through Columbine*, by JRW Case, 258 pgs., $18
*Without a Plea*, by Jeff Gundy, 96 pgs, $16
*Taking a Walk in My Animal Hat*, by Charlene Fix, 90 pgs, $16
*Earnest Occupations*, by Richard Hague, 200 pgs, $18
*Pieces: A Composite Novel*, by Mary Ann McGuigan, 250 pgs, $18
*Crows in the Jukebox: Poems*, by Mike James, 106 pgs, $16
*Portrait of the Artist as a Bingo Worker: A Memoir*, by Lori Jakiela, 216 pgs, $18
*The Thick of Thin: A Memoir*, by Larry Smith, 238 pgs, $18
*Cold Air Return: A Novel*, by Patrick Lawrence O'Keeffe, 390 pgs, $20
*Flesh and Stones: A Memoir*, by Jan Shoemaker, 176 pgs, $18
*Waiting to Begin: A Memoir*, by Patricia O'Donnell, 166 pgs, $18
*And Waking: Poems*, by Kevin Casey, 80 pgs, $16
*Both Shoes Off: Poems*, by Jeanne Bryner, 112 pgs, $16
*Abandoned Homeland: Poems*, by Jeff Gundy, 96 pgs, $16
*Stolen Child: A Novel*, by Suzanne Kelly, 338 pgs, $18

Bottom Dog Press, Inc.
P.O. Box 425 /Huron, Ohio 44839
http://smithdocs.net

## Books by Bottom Dog Press

### Harmony Series

*The Canary: A Novel*, by Michael Loyd Gray, 196 pgs, $18
*On the Flyleaf: Poems*, by Herbert Woodward Martin, 106 pgs, $16
*The Harmonist at Nightfall: Poems of Indiana*, by Shari Wagner, 114 pgs, $16
*Painting Bridges: A Novel*, by Patricia Averbach, 234 pgs, $18
*Ariadne & Other Poems*, by Ingrid Swanberg, 120 pgs, $16
*The Search for the Reason Why: New and Selected Poems*, by Tom Kryss, 192 pgs, $16
*Kenneth Patchen: Rebel Poet in America*, by Larry Smith, Revised 2nd Edition, 326 pgs, Cloth $28
*Selected Correspondence of Kenneth Patchen*, Edited with introduction by Allen Frost, Paper $18/ Cloth $28
*Awash with Roses: Collected Love Poems of Kenneth Patchen*, Eds. Laura Smith and Larry Smith with introduction by Larry Smith, 200 pgs, $16
*Breathing the West: Great Basin Poems*, by Liane Ellison Norman, 96 pgs, $16
*Maggot: A Novel*, by Robert Flanagan, 262 pgs, $18
*American Poet: A Novel*, by Jeff Vande Zande, 200 pgs, $18
*The Way-Back Room: Memoir of a Detroit Childhood*, by Mary Minock, 216 pgs, $18

Bottom Dog Press, Inc.
P.O. Box 425 /Huron, Ohio 44839
http://smithdocs.net

www.ingramcontent.com/pod-product-compliance
Lightning Source LLC
Chambersburg PA
CBHW021022090426
42738CB00007B/868